I'm Telling You!

Foreword

by

The Right Hon. Mr David Blunkett, MP

Secretary of State for Education and Employment

CAMBRIDGE
UNIVERSITY PRESS

PUBLISHED BY THE PRESS SYNDICATE OF THE UNIVERSITY OF CAMBRIDGE
The Pitt Building, Trumpington Street, Cambridge, United Kingdom

CAMBRIDGE UNIVERSITY PRESS
The Edinburgh Building, Cambridge CB2 2RU, UK   http://www.cup.cam.ac.uk
40 West 20th Street, New York, NY 10011–4211, USA http://www.cup.org
10 Stamford Road, Oakleigh, Melbourne 3166, Australia
Ruiz de Alarcón 13, 28014 Madrid, Spain

Illustrations © Lizzie Finlay 2000
Design by Angela Ashton

First published 2000

Printed in the United Kingdom at the University Press, Cambridge

Typeface Concorde *System* QuarkXpress®

A catalogue record for this book is available from the British Library

ISBN 0 521 78578 2 paperback

Contents

Foreword

by

The Right Hon. Mr David Blunkett, MP
Secretary of State for Education and Employment

I was very pleased to attend the awards ceremony for the recent Cambridge Young Writers competition. Competitions like this help to inspire young people to develop their writing skills and encourage children to write creatively.

I was particularly impressed by the way in which children can turn ordinary situations and experiences into interesting and sometimes hilarious stories.

The gift of a good writer is to open the door onto another world and inspire an enquiring mind. Good writing can provide companionship for the reader. The pleasure of writing down your own thoughts and dreams is a great freedom.

By learning to read, write and communicate confidently with other people, you not only increase your chances of doing well at school, but later in life when you leave school and start work.

The Young Writers competition organised by Cambridge University and Cambridge University Press fits with our National Literacy Strategy and with our work to encourage the whole community to help improve children's reading and writing skills. This work is continuing through the 'Read On' National Reading Campaign.

There is a wealth of literature that can fire the imagination. My earliest recollection of books was being read to by my mother, and then having learnt Braille, reading those, now politically incorrect books, like Enid Blyton and the Biggles stories which my generation absorbed greedily. But it was Jack London's novels about wolves and huskies, *The Call of the Wild* and *White Fang* , that really touched me in my teens. A combination of deep emotion, an awe of the glory and the cruelty of nature and my sentimentality about animals, combined to make a great impression on me.

A good book can inspire children to read more and to take up writing themselves. I hope all the children who read this book enjoy the stories as much as I did. I hope that it inspires all of you to use your imagination to write stories and share them with others.

London, December 1999

Mr Quine Dissects the Owl

by
Stacey Edmondson

It was the summer term and it was a very sunny day. We were playing out in the heat on the backfield. Andrea and Carrie were gossiping like usual and Jade was tagging along. They were in the far corner of the backfield when they came upon a dead baby tawny owl. It had been electrocuted! They quickly ran over the grass to where all the teachers were sitting drinking tea round the little white table.

It was 11.00 am when we got in from an extra long playtime. Mr Tansley told us when we were nicely lined up that he had rung Mr Quine and that Mr Quine was going to dissect the owl. The tables were outside the classroom and there were just two together in the middle of the junior classroom. On the tables was freshly laid newspaper and all of Mr Quine's instruments, plus the flopped dead owl.

We all stood round the two tables. Mr Tansley and Mr Quine walked into the room and my heart jumped. I felt squeamish which was strange because I'm not usually. I also felt excited. Mr Quine cut into a muscle and it landed on David's shoe! David didn't seem to mind. He just looked at it and shook his foot so it flew off. Everyone stepped back away from him and at next playtime no one dared go near him. They all said he had the owl germs. I felt sorry for him because everyone was picking on him.

We spent one hour dissecting the owl. When we had finished we went for lunch – turkey burgers. I felt sick and I couldn't eat because for a joke Mr Tansley had written 'owl burgers' on the menu. We still have the stuffed owl in the bike shed at school.

The Pirate

by
Vladimir Ivanov

Have you noticed that some parents do silly things at the most important moments of your life, usually at your birthday party?

They catch you off guard because you never thought that your parents – serious people – could do such silly, childish things. The worst thing is that they remember every detail of what happened and remind you of it constantly.

The story that I am going to tell you happened at my fifth birthday party. I had an enormous cake, dozens of balloons and all my family and friends were there.

I had just finished one of the most interesting books in the world, *Treasure Island* by Robert Louis Stevenson. It was really an unforgettable book. It made me dream of Captain Flint's treasure map and Long John Silver with his wooden leg. I was so impressed by this adventure that I wanted a birthday cake in the form of a treasure map.

The birthday party was in full swing. There was music and I was playing different games with my friends. Everyone was enjoying themselves. I was very happy when I opened my presents and discovered that I had got a train set, Game Boy, Lego and a lot of books. All the things I wanted.

I was so busy enjoying my new toys and books that I did not

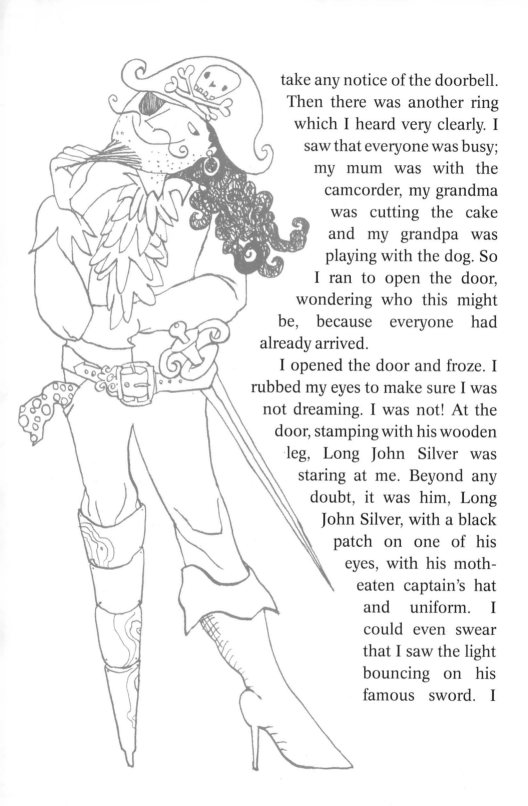

take any notice of the doorbell. Then there was another ring which I heard very clearly. I saw that everyone was busy; my mum was with the camcorder, my grandma was cutting the cake and my grandpa was playing with the dog. So I ran to open the door, wondering who this might be, because everyone had already arrived.

I opened the door and froze. I rubbed my eyes to make sure I was not dreaming. I was not! At the door, stamping with his wooden leg, Long John Silver was staring at me. Beyond any doubt, it was him, Long John Silver, with a black patch on one of his eyes, with his moth-eaten captain's hat and uniform. I could even swear that I saw the light bouncing on his famous sword. I could not move until he opened his mouth and said with a strange, deep and coarse voice, "Hello! Are you Vladimir?"

In the next second I ran as fast as a flash and dived under the bed in one of the bedrooms. Lying there, I was trying to be still as a rock. I held my breath, listening to what was going on, fearing that any second I would hear the taps of his wooden leg.

My grandparents' dog, who is one of my best friends, came immediately after me under the bed. He licked my face and looked puzzled that I was invading his usual sleeping territory.

I saw the door open and feared for the worst. Suddenly, I heard my mum's voice saying, "Vlad, Vlad, come out! Don't be afraid." The whole house rumbled with laughter.

All of a sudden I realised that the pirate was speaking with my dad's voice. Then, I remembered that my dad had disappeared from the party a few minutes before the pirate rang the doorbell. At last it dawned on me that the pirate was actually my father!

I came out from under the bed, angry, red with fury and stood in front of the pirate, pulled at his black patch, his hat and his crutch and shouted, "Why? Why are you making fun of me? Why are you so mean to me?" My father, laughing loudly, answered, "Vlad, I knew I would catch you this time. I was sure you would not recognise me under my perfect disguise. I even tied a piece of wood to my leg just to make it more realistic. I am sure that you will remember this birthday party for the rest of your life."

He was right. I still remember clearly every moment of it. Since then, before every birthday I wonder what surprise my parents have cooked up.

The Day I Walked in Wet Cement

by

Bryan Clark

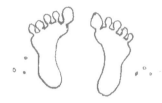

When I was six, I was going to the shop, in Skegness. I stood in wet cement and I was there for half an hour. By now the cement was drying and I got worried.

The shop assistant came out and tried to help me.

It was no use. She could not get me out.

My dad was wondering where I was and he came over! My dad had an idea and he pulled my shoes off and I got out.

I thanked him all day.

My First Day at School

by

Abigail Connor

My first day at school was very frightening because when I walked into the classroom everyone looked at me like I was someone out of space. I was very nervous. I thought that I would start crying. I was standing there with my mum and everyone was looking at me. My mum left and I was still standing there like a statue. My belly was dry and rumbling.

Then this tall teacher stood up and said, "Claire, take Abigail and show her where to put her coat." This girl stood up. I was so nervous I couldn't even move a foot. She took my hand and led me down a long hall. I was led to a peg. On the peg my name was printed with big letters ABIGAIL CONNOR. It was amazing; I was a part of the school already.

When I had been in school for a few weeks, I felt part of the school and I had lots of friends. Now I am a year three!

The Great Ear Piercing

by
Sarah Smith

It all started a long time before the event, when my friend Zoë asked me, "Why don't you get your ears pierced?"

'Me?' I thought. 'My ears are fine! Why tamper with them?'

"Well?" pressed Zoë. "Are you going to?"

"I don't think so," I replied slowly. "Does it hurt?"

"Not much," she assured me. "Please do it."

"I'll think about it," I replied.

Did God intend us to have holes in our ears? I pondered the question.

The next time I gave it some thought, however, was a month later. I had seen girls with their ears pierced and I thought it looked quite pleasant. The only thing that bothered me was the pain.

"Does it hurt?" I asked many girls.

"Not much," they replied.

I nearly screamed. What kind of answer was that?

"Mum," I asked, "why can't you have an anaesthetic for ear piercing?"

"Don't be silly!" she replied. "An anaesthetic would just be another needle in your ear!"

Finally, feeling rather unsure, I decided to do it. Mum and I went to town on Saturday and booked it for the Thursday at 1.00 pm. The place I was booked at was inviting and airy, with mirrors and comfy chairs. However, I wasn't relaxed when it came to Thursday.

It was a bright day with some pearly clouds stretched across the sky. I felt as though nothing would ever be the same again as we walked down a little dark alleyway into a range of shops called the Peacock Mews. I remember seeing a café and wondering whether Mum would take me there when we came out. And then we were there.

We found the shop and asked the woman at the counter when it would be done.

"Right now," she answered. "I'll just fetch Belinda." Belinda was curling hair at the back of the shop.

"Belinda," she called, "there's a girl here who wants her ears done."

"I'm just coming," replied Belinda.

She came over. She had black hair and dangly scissor earrings.

"How long have you done this?" questioned Mum.

"About fourteen years," she answered.

Mum nodded, satisfied.

Then Belinda showed me some studs, all different shapes and sizes.

"Something plain," suggested Mum. "Something you can wear to school." She pointed some out; triangles, squares and a few circles. I chose the circles.

Belinda sat me down on a black leather swinging chair and took a Biro from her desk. Then she swung me round so I could see my ears in the mirror and marked two blue dots.

"About there do you think?" she questioned.

"OK," I mumbled.

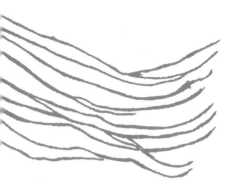

I felt apprehensive and scared. The trouble was I couldn't imagine the pain. I never can. I just get a horrible, lurching feeling in my stomach.

She took something like a stapler from a drawer. She carefully placed the parts in it and then said,

"On the count of 3; …1 …2 …3!"

The pain was incredible. It was all I could do not to tear at my own ears and before I could say Jack Robinson she had done the other. Strangely enough, however, it was not the sort of pain that made you want to cry. It was a disbelief that anything could hurt like that. I just couldn't remember how it felt to have painless ears.

"Are you all right?" Mum asked, anxiously.

"I'm fine," I replied, a little dazed.

I looked in the mirror. My face (bright red) looked like a tomato! But I was pleased. Belinda dabbed some cream on my ears to cool them. Ears stinging but head upright I proudly emerged from the shop.

Bug Boy of the Day!

by

James Richardson

I woke up feeling terrified that we had to depart to Disney's Animal Kingdom which was in Orlando, Florida. It was a boiling 72 degrees. We had breakfast and then we staggered to the bus stop. When the bus eventually came, it was full and we had to stand. It was hot and stuffy and it felt terrible.

When we arrived at Animal Kingdom, I almost fell out of the bus because I was so tired. After a short walk to the entrance, we were even hotter than before. It was now a toasting 75 degrees. When we finally stopped, I felt so exhausted that I couldn't go another step. When Mum and Dad finally got me to go, we went straight to the train station which took us to a mysterious part of the park. It was called the Conservation Station. On the train I kept on thinking 'Be brave, be brave.' When the train pulled into the station I nearly got my foot trapped in the rails.

We got out of the station and I saw a drink stand. I looked at it with delight and thought, 'I'll ask my mum and dad if I can buy a drink.' I asked them and they replied, "James you only had your breakfast an hour ago." "But, but," I pleaded. "No James! We've got better things to do than to keep buying drinks."

After that unsettlement I had to hang on for a drink.

When we finally got to this mysterious place, I felt as if I was in heaven. It was so beautifully decorated and there was so much technology. There were so many computers and so much wildlife. While I was studying a computer my mum grabbed me by the shoulder and pulled me to where my dad and brother were sitting. Dad said, "A show is going to start in a minute or two."

When the representatives finally came I was shocked because on one of the boxes that they were carrying it had printed in big, bold letters 'DANGER! Carnivorous Animals Inside.'

I felt as if something had just bitten me. The lady representative spoke and she asked a question. The question was, "Does anybody know where a tarantula would live because we lost one when we came in?"

I froze still with fright. Then after a long pause I spoke. I answered in a shivery voice, "Is it behind where I'm sitting?" The lady came over. She searched and searched, then finally she found it, but there was nothing to worry about. It was only pretend! Everybody laughed and laughed!

Suddenly the man asked, "Does anybody want to come up here?" Everybody was as still as a statue. Then I said in a determined voice, "I will." I went up onto the stage. When I was on the stage the lady asked, "Will you put these glasses on?" But I couldn't answer. She had already put them on me. The glasses felt as if I had bug eyes and eyebrows.

Then the man reached for a box. I kept on thinking, 'Please make it be friendly!' In the box that the man pulled out there was a tarantula (and this time it wasn't pretend!). Then the lady asked me, "Will you hold it?" After a short pause, I answered, "Yes, I will." When I was holding it, it felt really hairy and it kept on touching me with its hairy legs. It felt as if I was holding an extremely hairy man's chest. Then the man asked, "Does anybody know where a scorpion lives?"

Suddenly my brother answered, "Behind me!" It was only a pretend one, but while the man was doing that, the lady went and got another box which had a real scorpion in it. When the man had finished, the lady gave me the scorpion to hold. The scorpion felt hard and spiky. It felt as if I had spikes stuck in my hands. When I put my hands together, the scorpion and tarantula fought like mad! The tarantula kept spitting poison at the scorpion, then the scorpion tried to sting the tarantula but missed. "OH!" I screamed.

Then the lady put the tarantula and scorpion back in their boxes and said, "Give James a round of applause." Then she came up to me and took the glasses off me and said, "James you are the Bug Boy of the Day." I was amazed.

When the show was over, Mum, Dad and Matthew asked me, "Was that good?" I replied, "It was OK." When we were on the train I was still amazed she'd called me Bug Boy of the Day. When we left the park, the bus wasn't busy but when we got to our room I was exhausted. Then my mum said that we were going to the EPCOT Centre the next day!

I didn't say it out loud, but I thought, 'OH NO.'

The Girl Gang

by
Emily Dickson

"I want a blood test and a CT scan of your head please," said Mr Sargent. I felt my whole body go totally stiff. I am petrified of needles. I put on a brave face and went to the nurse. She showed me the needle, it looked about ten inches long. I wasn't going to let her take my blood! I sat on my arm and told her it was child abuse. The nurse gave up and suggested we ask my own doctor to do it. I felt cross and I couldn't really understand why I had to have the blood test.

I woke the next morning feeling rather scared and we went straight to the doctor. When we got there, they kept us waiting for what seemed like hours. The nurse was not at all sympathetic and the needle seemed even longer than last time. I sat on my arm again. This made the nurse get angry and made me cry. Again we went home without the blood test being done. Mum phoned Mr Sargent to ask if the blood test was essential. He said to have my CT scan and see what the results were.

My scan was done a couple of days later. I was a little apprehensive but I had to go. I had to put my head against a piece of hard plastic to hold it steady and then stay completely still which wasn't too hard really. An enormous disc went round and round my head; it sounded like a washing machine. The scan took about twenty minutes and then a man came out and said my brain was fine and that we could go home.

We waited about a week for the results. Mr Sargent said that I had some fluid in my mastoid but he did not want to do another mastoidectomy in case my hearing deteriorated even more. It was a big relief! Mr Sargent made an appointment for Dr Day to see me at Pembury Hospital, for he could do no more. He did not think that the problems with my ears were causing me to be so ill. I felt as though nobody knew what was wrong with me and yet I still kept on feeling very tired, having really bad headaches and losing weight.

I did not want to go and see Dr Day because I was sure the question of the blood test would raise its ugly head again. Mum agreed with me because she said she thought it unlikely he would find anything physically wrong with me. She talked to me for a long time about stress. Mum told me that if you are suffering from stress it could make you physically ill, that it could give you bad headaches, make you feel tired and cause you to lose weight. She asked me if anything was worrying me either at home or at school. Then I really spilled the beans. I told her how most of the girls in my class were being hateful to me, how they excluded me from all their games and told other people not to play with me. I told her how lonely my days were at school and how I spent the play times on my own. Mum was very upset and asked why I had not told her before what was going on. This was hard to explain but I think I didn't want to give her any more worries because my brother had been seriously ill and both Mum and Dad were very concerned about him. He was still unable to go to school and was often very poorly.

Mum went to see the teachers at school and told them what had been going on. They said that I should come back to school and that they would make quite sure there was no more bullying. I had had many weeks off school by this time and was frightened about going back but I thought it would be for the best. With a lot of encouragement from Mum and Dad I went back to school. I was worried that people would ask me what had been wrong with me and that I did not have an answer to give them. I should have realised most of them wouldn't even think to ask. They just got stuck straight into bullying me again.

On my first day back we did a science experiment in groups of six and the results were put on the classroom wall with all our names on it. By the end of the day my name had been scribbled off the list. I felt so hurt, I felt as if someone had bitten a chunk out of my heart. I felt cold and weird but I decided to take no notice of them. The next day I tried to start afresh and pretend nothing had upset me. At break I went to play with my friends, but they just turned away. The hole in my heart grew. I went home that day feeling very tired and ill. I ate a little dinner and went to bed. In the morning I could not get up. I told Mum everything that had happened and she was very cross. Mum went to see my teacher again! The teacher said that she would speak to the leaders of the gang concerned and that nothing bad would happen to me again. I trusted my teacher so I went back to school the next day, but the girls all laughed at me. They said that they were going to kick my head in and if I dared to tell my mum or the teachers again they would kick my head in anyway. They bullied me until I was screaming inside. I thought nobody would ever like me, that it was all my fault and that there must be something wrong with me which made people hate me.

When I came home in a state again, Mum and Dad decided to give up with the school and move me to another one. At first I did not want to go. I felt even more scared. I thought the same things would happen all over again. Mum and Dad thought

Fosse Bank was a lovely school and that it would suit me perfectly so they tried very hard to encourage me to go there. I slept on it and in the morning I had a look at the prospectus with Mum and I decided it looked like an excellent school.

Mum arranged for me to look round and I really liked the atmosphere in Fosse Bank. It felt so friendly, I felt at home straight away. Mum and Dad liked it too, so in September I started there. I loved it from the first day. Everyone was so friendly and kind to me and they made me feel very welcome. After the first week I realised all my symptoms were disappearing and I felt fine. Dad said I was eating so much he didn't think he could afford to keep me much longer! I could see that he was happy about it though and was only joking. So Mum was right, all my illness was caused by stress!

A True Life Experience

by
Amie McLaughlin

One day, when I was about seven, my nan came around my house because my mum was going to work. I asked whether I could have my hamster out, but my nan said, "No." I threw myself on the floor and screamed my head off. As I was screaming, my sister Emily came in the room. She giggled, called me a baby and ran out of the room. When she went out I screamed and cried even more. My nan came in to settle me down, but I would not take it and started kicking her. In the end she went downstairs with Emily to watch a video.

I was alone. This was my chance to get the hamster down myself. I went into my room and climbed onto the top bunk. I grabbed the cage, climbed down from the bed and put the cage on the floor. I got Tom the hamster out and played with him, letting him run around the room. I did this for quite a while, then I got bored so I put him back in the cage and, as I was in such a strop, I forgot to close the cage door.

I went downstairs to watch TV. Nan said to me, "Have you calmed down now?" I did not answer because I knew I would get in trouble if she found out. When my mum got home I had a bath. When I got out Mum said to me, "Why is the cage down?"

'Uh oh,' I thought. "Nan said I could!" I said. Mum said no more. I knew I was guilty, but I could not tell the truth.

In the morning, my mum came in my room. She didn't look happy. "What's wrong Mum?" I said with a cheeky smile. My mum replied, "Your hamster has gone away for a while." I said, "What, on holiday?" I knew what she was going on about but I could not admit it. Then I started to cry. My dad came upstairs and said that I couldn't have another one. I cried even more, but it didn't work – he was gone, my poor mate Tom. I knew he was dead because I found his left-overs in the cat's bowl.

About five months later I got a new hamster – I think I was lucky!

Bike Boy

by
Craig Parry

Over the Easter holidays I decided that I was going to learn to ride my bike. So I got the bike out of the shed and I asked my dad to take my stabilisers off, which he did.

I jumped on it, so excited! I pushed off . . . and what do you think happened? Yes, I fell to the ground!

I was not badly bruised. I picked myself up and glanced at my dad. He was smiling a little bit but I wasn't annoyed with him.

Dad gave me an idea. He said that I should push off with my foot on one pedal and then pick the other foot up onto the other pedal. Then I should try to ride. I did this. He helped me at first by running behind.

I kept on trying and trying. In fact I did it so much that I broke one of my pedals! That meant I couldn't ride my bike any more that day.

The next day, when Dad came home from work, he had new pedals and he put them on the bike for me. And I started again.

After I had fallen off a couple of times Dad said, "Why don't you go outside the gate and down the road?"

We went down the road as far as the bridge and Dad said that I was getting better, so we rode all the way back home.

Dad had to go to football training but I just couldn't stop now!

I thought I'd try on my own. I climbed up onto the seat and pushed on the pedal and what do you think happened? I kept my balance all the way from one end of the yard to the other! I couldn't believe it! I was SO excited I went running into the house calling, "Mummy, Mummy, come and see! I can ride my bike!"

She came out and I did it again. I fell off before I reached the gate this time but Mummy was so proud she gave me a big round of applause.

And now I can ride my bike whenever and wherever I like!

My First Win

by
Ellie Ragdale

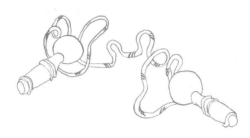

At Home

It was the day of the Infants Sports Day in 1996. I was entering the skipping and running races. I was at home getting ready for school.

"Would you like to take your skipping rope?" Mum asked.

"No, thank you," I replied. I was nervous as this was my first Sports Day and I was excited.

"Will you be coming to school?" I asked Mum.

"Yes, and Dad can come too."

I was pleased my dad could come. We live in a Youth Hostel so my dad is busy most of the time.

Nervous

It was the afternoon. Everyone was getting ready for the Sports Day and I was now even more nervous. Mrs Bailey, my teacher, came into the room.

"Everyone line up," she shouted. We all went outside. I saw some mums and dads on chairs. I knew that my mum and dad would soon come to watch me.

Run, Run, Run

I lined up for the running race. I wasn't very nervous because I knew that Caroline or Denise would win.

"On your marks, get set, go!"

We were off! We ran. At last I reached the finish line. I think I must have been fourth. Everyone clapped and I was pleased with myself.

The Skipping Race

Now I was nervous. I grabbed my rope and lined up next to Michelle.

"On your marks, get set, go!"

I was going well. I'm a good skipper and so is Michelle. My heart was beating madly. The distance seemed to be about thirty metres long (it probably was). I was about twenty metres from the finishing line when I heard Holly (my sister) calling. Then I saw that Michelle was in front of me!

Faster, Faster

I was worried. I really wanted to win this race. I wished Michelle would slow down. She did. I think she must have got tangled up. I glanced round. Good! Now it was my chance. I skipped faster. I didn't see if she had got faster. Only ten more skips to go.

I've done it

I had won the race. I was so surprised and thrilled. The crowd clapped. I sat through the rest of Sports Day feeling wonderful but tired.

Grin

I wore my sticker, to show that I was a winner, and a big grin. I was so pleased that I had won THE SKIPPING RACE!!!

Best Friends

by
Rachel Beagrie

It was a long autumn day. The leaves fell on my head as I stood watching the children playing in the playground. I felt very left out, like a child with no past and no future. I had no friends at all. As the sun dimmed and we went in, I felt horrible. Then I collected my bag and went home with all the other children.

The next day we came back to school. I sat down on a bench and waited for the bell to ring. But then I saw two children I'd never seen before. I walked up to them and asked if I could play with them. "Yes," they said.

I was delighted at what I'd heard. I had two new best friends. I was never going to be lonely again. 'Yippie!' I thought, 'I've found two friends at last.'

And I still have those two friends today.

Owen's Calamity

by
Huw Silk

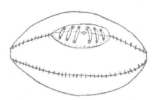

Owen woke earlier than usual and slammed me over the head with his plastic axe. Huh! Who invented little brothers?

"Huw, Huw it's time for breakfast, 'cos it's the match later!"

I groaned. How could I forget?

"Coosh on oo welp," Owen exclaimed, through a mouthful of Cinnamon Grahams.

"Pardon?" I asked.

Owen swallowed and replied, "I'm supporting Wales, come on you Welsh."

He kept on repeating those lines, through his toast, egg and bacon.

"BE QUIET," I eventually roared at him.

It didn't stop him. The only thing that did stop him was the referee's shrill whistle as we settled down on our plastic chairs. The men behind didn't look too pleased with Dad (well who does like Owen's singing?). Dad survived for seventy of the eighty minutes, though.

The Arms Park went wild. Arwel Thomas's kick pierced a hole in the gap between the posts.

Everyone rose to their feet. Owen clambered onto his seat and WHEEEEE! He slipped down the back of his seat!

"Get up," Dad called down at my little brother.

"I can't Dad, I can't." Dad pulled Owen's arms and sure enough he was stuck fast.

For the remaining ten minutes more attention was paid to Owen's calamity than the game. A group of Aussies around us joined in the pulling and, when the final whistle finally blew, all the noise and colour drained from the Arms Park.

Dad alerted three stewards to the situation. Two of them helped us and the third went to fetch a screwdriver. They pulled for a quarter of an hour, without success!

Then I went for walkies. How embarrassing this was.

CRRRRAAAACK!

I dropped the newspaper I was reading and an ant I had picked up probably died of shock. I turned round and galloped towards the sound. Then I saw something which made my heart leap. Owen was free!

But I saw the dismal look on their faces. One of the stewards had his feet waggling around in the air. He had pulled Owen so hard that, when Owen popped out, the steward shot back into the row behind, head-first, and was now screaming for help. UH-OH!!!

37

Learning To Swim

by
Tom Risdon

"No, I don't want to go!" I yelled at my mum fiercely. "Well you've got to go, to learn how to swim properly," my mum replied, suprisingly calmly. "I won't, I won't, I won't, I won't!" I hung onto the seat for dear life. There was no way I was going into the pool in Eversfield. But, as always, my mum's tireless efforts prevailed and I was in a long hallway leading to the swimming pool. I looked around as I stood there waiting, my body trembling with both excitement and fear. I jumped as someone came round the corner.

"Hello," the man said cheerfully. "My name's Charlie Brown. And you are?" I looked up at his beaming face. "Tom," I said. Maybe this wasn't so bad after all. "Follow me." He walked briskly around the corner and I had to run after him! He suddenly stopped and pointed to a door. I spelt out the sign, G-E-N-T-L-E-M-E-N it said. "That's where you change," he said. I opened the door and walked in. I was the first person to arrive. There was a musty smell and the floor was cold and damp.

When I had changed I was led into a room with a large pool in it. It was not huge, but it was very attractive, as someone had painted huge murals of swimmers and people jumping off the diving board. Another wall was completely glass and there were two huge statues on either side of the door. This pool belonged to a private house and the owners allowed small groups from the local schools to take lessons there, so we were very lucky. The owner's two terrier dogs used to wander into the changing rooms and caused quite a commotion and amusement amongst us boys. They used to pinch our shoes and socks so we had to go tearing after them before they reached the forbidden territory of the main house.

"Climb down the steps," said Charlie enthusiastically. I gave out a squeal as I put my foot in the icy water. Circles appeared where I put my foot in. Fascinated, I dabbled my toes in the water. Then I flung myself into the clear blue liquid with a SPLASH!

I pulled my head up hurriedly. My belly was stinging. It was then I discovered what it felt like in a swimming pool. It was cold, it was painful if you hit it and it stung your eyes.

Suddenly there was a massive splash and Charlie was beside me. All the other children were also scrambling in. There was James, Chris, William, Jonathan and Lewis. Charlie told us to line up at the end of the pool. We were about to begin our first lesson. Charlie was going to teach us how to float on our backs. He demonstrated. He lent back in the water and lifted his legs and suddenly he was floating. It all looked easy and so effortless, but it certainly wasn't. Time after time I sank to the bottom like a brick. Coughing and spluttering I tried again and again but no. Everyone else seemed to be doing it, why couldn't I? Suddenly I felt a firm hand underneath me and there was Charlie, supporting me and telling me what to do. Just as suddenly the firm hand left me and once again I sank to the bottom. This was hopeless. I was never going to swim.

Now Charlie was handing out bright orange armbands which we all had to inflate and pull on. This was better! At last I was able to keep my head above water. I thrashed my legs

around in the water furiously. Suddenly I was moving forward – was I now swimming? I couldn't quite believe it! I was moving through the water like a cruiser. Slowly and laboriously I made it across the pool without sinking. I let out a cry of delight as I looked across at the distance I had travelled. It was quite a long way for a beginner but Charlie made us do it again and again until the end of the lesson. I was growing more and more confident each time. When the session finally came to an end Charlie congratulated us all as we left with our smiling mothers.

After each lesson came fun time. Charlie let us play with the balls and floats and flippers. This was the time we liked the most and Charlie sometimes joined in too, giving us piggy backs and playing catch.

This went on for some weeks until … the big day arrived. We were no longer given armbands to wear. My heart sank. How was I going to manage without them? One by one we were told to swim alone across the pool with Charlie keeping watch. I was first in the line and stood there shivering and feeling very nervous and apprehensive. Was I going to make it or was I going to sink? Off I went, flapping my arms wildly trying to keep my head above water. I felt myself sinking slowly and I kicked my legs frantically trying to keep afloat. My eyes were stinging and my mouth kept filling with water. I was spluttering and choking and I began to panic. Desperately I thrashed my legs in the water. I was sure I was drowning. It was all such a struggle and I could hardly breathe. Suddenly I heard my friends yelling, "Come on Tom, you're nearly there." With one huge effort I ploughed through the water to find that I had reached the other side safely. I had made it! I could swim!

"Yippee," I cried. I felt great. All the hard work had been worth it. I felt that I had done something brilliant. I had achieved my goal – I had learnt how to swim.

Autobiography

by

Balvinder Atmi

I was born on 6th June 1989 in Kabul in Afghanistan. It was a very happy day for my parents. This story is set in Afghanistan where my whole family lived together – my grandpa, grandma, my mother and me. We were all living very happily. My grandpa used to bring a lot of toffees, chocolates and toys for me. We were all living very happily. We were called a happy family.

After five years, mountains of sorrow had fallen on us. On 10th May 1995 our house was surrounded by terrorists. They had come to our place and my grandpa was shot and died on the spot. They took me from my mother and asked for gold and money.

My parents managed to give it to them in two days.

But for two days I was with the terrorists in the jungle, crying and very hungry. After two days they met my parents again and took the money and gold. I was back with my family.

After six days, my brother Jaitinder was born into the world of sorrow. My parents were very depressed that we couldn't celebrate that day and my grandpa was no more to bring toffees, chocolates and toys for my brother.

After two years we left Afghanistan with all the sweet memories of my grandpa and my happy life.

A Boring Day

by
Scott Phillips

Just imagine one warm shady day in February. There's not a thing to do. Your football has been punctured and there is not anything amusing on the telly – well not until half past three.

I was playing with my friends in our street. Oh, did I tell you my friends' names? They are Stephen and Michael, our next door neighbours. Suddenly my mum bobbed out of the door quite merrily and came up to me.

The Movie

"Scott," she said, "do you want to go to the cinema to see A Bug's Life?"

"Yes please," I replied.

"We will go tonight at 8 o'clock sharp."

Five Hours Later

"Scott," said Mum in a disappointed fashion, "we could not get tickets for A Bug's Life, but if we take a chance we might get tickets for A Bug's Life in Aylesbury."

In Aylesbury

We are in Aylesbury now. "Mum," I said, "do you know where we can park?"

"We will park in the multi-storey car park, Scott," said Mum.

In the Car Park

"Will Mum be back soon Dad?" I said. Suddenly Mum came back flapping the tickets above her head.

After the movie we came back and stopped dead in our tracks. It was our worst nightmare, we were frozen, staring in disbelief.

Oh, no!

The car park was shut!

"Oh, no," said Dad. There were gates all around the car park. I put my head in my hands as I saw a notice. This is what it said:

WARNING. *This car park shuts at 20.00 hours*

"We will get the car out in the morning," sighed Dad. "We can get a train," I suggested. "Good idea," Dad said.

When we got to the station there was another notice saying there were no more trains that night. I felt awful. "Let's go to the bus station," said Dad. So off we went on another mission.

No more buses.

"What kind of town is this?" shouted Dad. "There is only one more choice," said Dad. "A cab."

"Oh, no Dad," I said as I saw a cab with a scary-looking man inside it.

"How much to Leighton Buzzard?" Dad asked. "£12.00," said the man. We hopped into the smoky air inside the cab. I was so relieved when I saw our street. I ran in through our door and hugged the dog. I was home.

Friends Forever

by
Ellen Matkins

"Sa, Sa," I gurgled to my friend Sarah when I was very small. "Ah, aren't they adorable," said my mum warmly.

You see, when I was born, my mum and her best friend, Jill, had their children round about the same time, so they would visit each other quite often and bring us babies with them. That's how Sarah and I grew up to be best friends. Very best friends. Celia, my twin sister, found a girl called Linsey, who went to the same school, to be her best friend.

As time went on Sarah and I went to the same playgroup and school as each other. We had all that best friends could want.

Until one night when my mother was in the kitchen. My dad wasn't feeling at all right, so he went into the garage and picked up a mallet, dragged it back into the kitchen and swiped my mum over the head with it.

I didn't hear any of it. I just found myself being woken up by my Irish uncle, my dad's brother. My dad didn't have the accent but he did!

"Daddy?" I called. "No, it's ya Uncle Harry," he called back. He had entered my room and some light shone in, but I only could make out the black hair, so I assumed it was Dad.

Downstairs there were policemen at every door, making sure

they were kept shut. I didn't understand and I don't think my brother or sister did either.

"Come on Ellen, go and find your slippers," said Harry in a hurry. "Where's Mummy?" I asked Harry. "Oh, your mummy's had a little accident. Now come on!"

I thought my slippers were in the garage, but to get to the garage you had to go through the kitchen. I tried to get round the policeman, but I then understood that he didn't want me to get through! In the end I found the slippers somewhere else.

We got into Uncle Harry's car and he drove us back to his house. We went to bed in the lounge, with a sheet under us and a sheet, thin as paper, on top. Cold as it was, I got to sleep in the end.

In the morning we were curious about what had happened, but all they would say was, "Your mummy's had a little accident!" Later we were taken up to Grandma and Grandpa's house. We call them Mamma and Daddit. My brother invented the names when we were little and we've called them that ever since.

We stayed there for a few nights, then found that a year floated by when we were there. I felt I would die. We did visit Mummy sometimes, but all there was to see was a person who I wasn't sure was Mum, covered with tubes, with a hole in her neck which the doctors called a tracheotomy, which helped her breathe. Then another time when I saw her, she had half her hair shaved off and was being fed porridge through her nose.

"Oh I want to see Mummy!" I bawled. It had started when Mamma (Grandma) told me my mother was staying with her friend Jane. We hadn't seen Mummy for a month.

I felt my life was a dream just fading slowly away. The only communication with my dad was letters and they hardly said a lot.

Then my mother moved back into our house, but we remained at Mamma's. Every Saturday we would travel the miles back to visit Mummy. At last she moved in with us at Mamma's and soon found a suitable house for us all to live in. It was just about half a mile down the road from Mamma's.

We were planning to keep going to Hartley school but, because it was so far away, we had to go to the local school in Chiddingstone. I was missing my best friend Sarah a great deal, for I was six now and it was actually one whole year that we had spent staying at Mamma's and Daddit's.

Mummy wasn't allowed to drive because the wounds on her face were bad and one eye was blinded, so that meant Mamma had to drive us. We lived now in our new house by the green in Chiddingstone Hoath. Chiddingstone and the school was just about two miles down the road. In Hartley, our school was just around the corner.

"There's going to be a maypole dance soon," Mamma said as we drew near to the school gates. I watched some girls who looked quite a few years older than me, dancing round a maypole in the front garden. Me and my sister Celia were speechless. I don't think Alex, my one year older brother, was too happy either.

We came home to find a jaffa cake waiting in a bare kitchen for us. We had the house made clear of woodworm and I found I had to share a room with Celia; I mean what would you expect with twins?

"Owww!" screamed Celia. "Haaa Haaa!" I yelled back. Celia had been laughing at me for about two minutes now, so I had scratched her. She was laughing because when those four words came up, "FIRST DAY OF SCHOOL" she had to remember what happened that first morning. For as we got out of the car, a man, now known to me as THE man, came waddling down the path with three dogs at his side. My grandma obviously knew him because of the look on her face, "Oh hello, these are my grandchildren Celia and Ellen, they're twins." "Oh, you'd never have noticed," he said with a surprised look on his rather small face.

I suddenly felt a warm wet tingle on my foot and then to my horror found that one of his dogs was weeing on me! "Mamma, Mamma," I had said, but when I told them they just chuckled. Celia was now teasing me about it and I felt like a piece of old, ripped up newspaper being chucked on the fire. Well she had really got me up in flames this time.

Sarah would never laugh that horribly at me, ever. I was getting desperate, I needed to see my old school.

Oh my! Then one day through the post came a parcel for me. It was a dear little children's poetry book from my old school. In the book was written:

Dear Ellen,

We all hope that you are having a happy time in your new school and that you will enjoy this book.

From
all of your friends at Hartley School xxx.

A tear fell from my eye, "Oh but I miss you," I quietly said to myself.

Celia got a story book and Alex got a science book. I only wrote to Sarah about two to three times a month. Oh yes! We did see each other because Mummy met up with Jill every so often.

Cards and posies fled though the door like today's the last day.

"No, no, no, no!" Father he, he, he's dead.

My dad was found to have strangled himself. It was probably all my fault, because about three months ago we visited the jail hospital which he was staying in. He probably got so upset with what had happened he felt life just wasn't worth living.

'Bye Dad.

The funeral cut my heart.

Our house was fixed up, and all we needed to do now was decorate. With all the fighting me and Celia had done we had to be separated, and quick!

"Right Ellen, you are going to live in my room now and I'm going down to the playroom."

Now we have a better life and out of all our bad luck we had to have a bit of good luck, so using nearly all the snowdrops in the country, I wished one sensible and good wish. That even if Mummy doesn't marry him, I hope she finds a man just to help her.

Me and Sarah can now be good friends forever, even from a distance.

The Race

by

Laura Lambert

I'm going to tell you what happened to me last week. My family and I went to my nan's house in the country. I hear you saying, "What is so amazing about that?" I went to do a junior run, a very long run! I've done lots of races before, but they were short, quick ones. This one was long and slow. What if I sprint off quickly at the beginning, and get tired too quickly? These thoughts hung in my head.

We went down to my nan's house to stay the night before. After my favourite tea cooked by my nan, I played cards with my granddad. He beat me, and I began to worry again that all the other children would beat me in the race tomorrow.

"Time for bed! You must have an early night if you are going to run well tomorrow," said Dad.

I slowly got ready for bed thinking all the time about tomorrow. I imagined that all I could see were crowds of people laughing at me because I finished last, hours and hours after everybody else.

All night I tossed and turned; I didn't get a wink of sleep. All I could hear was laughter and shouting.

Next morning at breakfast time my dad asked me, "What are you so worked up about, you've done races before?" But he didn't understand. I tried to force some breakfast down my tight throat but I couldn't eat anything. I became full very quickly. "You'll have to eat something if you're going to run," said Dad. Nan looked at me as if she understood my feelings.

I went upstairs to the room I was sleeping in. It seemed dark, very dark, like a shadow had passed over it. There in the darkest of corners was a chair with my running things on it. 'OH, NO!' I thought to myself. I walked over. I felt like I was being led to the unknown. Then it came.

Dad shouted, "Laura we're going in about fifteen minutes so hurry up." I felt my heart jump. I didn't want to hurry, I wanted to go as slow as possible. But something, a sort of energy inside me, said, "Go on, hurry up! We don't want to be late do we?" It kept on saying it over and over again. I seemed to want to do as it said so I got dressed quickly. When I was dressed I went to clean my teeth. I looked at myself in the mirror. Staring back at me wasn't the usual face I'd seen many times before. This one was a different face I didn't know. A face that had been somewhere that no other had been.

Mum came in at that point with a hair brush. I could tell it was going to be one of her morning quick brush jobs. I didn't want her to do one of those brushes, firstly because they hurt and secondly it would go too quickly. Mum was talking to me about something or other but I wasn't listening. My stomach felt like it had a mind of it's own, tying itself in knots. Mum kept asking me if I was all right and if I had been to the toilet. Mothers are SO annoying! Eventually Mum finished putting my hair into two tails with matching ribbons.

Dad started shouting. He was getting excited I could tell. "Come on everybody, time to go, we don't want to be late!" 'Don't we?' I thought. It was now getting difficult to walk. Nan came along and held my hand and helped me into the car and she sat next to me and kept winking at me. On the radio the song with the words "It can only get better" was playing; it kept going over and over in my head. Dad drove far too quickly and we arrived far too early.

When we got there Dad went to look for the toilet. Perhaps he was nervous as well! I was shaking uncontrollably when Nan looked at me and asked, "What's wrong?" I looked up at her and said, "I'm so tired and nervous, I didn't get a wink of sleep last night." Nan listened carefully to every word. She hugged me and whispered in my ear, "If you finish the race first or last I'll give you £10." "Wow!" I said. That certainly made me feel a whole lot better.

Dad returned from the toilets and from the registration desk with my race number. He pinned it onto my vest and suggested that we started warming up. Dad's race started first. He kissed me and wished me luck before lining up with the other marathon runners. When his race gun went off I jumped out of my skin and shook for a whole minute. Mum laughed and hugged me tight.

The announcer called, "Five minutes to the children's race." 'Oh no,' I thought, 'I'm going to be sick!' Nan took control. She led me to the start, hugged me and said, "Remember, £10 for a finish!" 'Yes,' I thought, 'I want that.'

The race official said, "On your marks, get set, GO!" Bang went the gun. We were off. At first it seemed that all the runners were coming past me and I was going backwards but I knew how far we had to run and that to go too quick at the beginning was not good. I started to feel much better; all my training was beginning to pay off. I concentrated on the race and to this day I don't know where we were running. I just looked at the mile markers and counted them down.

I was now overtaking runners. Some had stopped and were walking holding their sides. I thought to myself, 'They've got a stitch.' I was really feeling much better now; I was catching a really big boy who had left the start like a rocket. The race sign said 250 m to go. "Come on," I said to myself, "catch him, catch him!" Slowly, slowly I caught him up. Oh no, there's the finish. I'm not going to beat him. Come on! My legs were getting very tired but I really tried to go faster and faster and the finish was getting closer and closer. COME ON!

On the line I overtook him into first place.

"Yes!" I cried and put my arms in the air. Mum and Nan were jumping up and down hugging each other. The race official gave me my medal and the photographer took my picture. Mum ran up and hugged me and said she was so proud, but my nan just winked and slipped a folded ten pound note into my hand.

Stuck in a Lift

by
Shankara Oakes

When I was five years old I got stuck in a lift!

It all started like this . . .

I was on holiday in America with my three brothers, Connor, Jordan and Oliver and my mum. We were staying in a hotel which had a lift. It could fit about five people in and it had a big mirror on the wall. We had been using this lift nearly all holiday to get from our room to other places.

We were going down for breakfast one day and Connor pressed the button for the lift. When the lift came, we got in but, just then, two more people came and they got in too. These people were strangers – a man and a woman. At first it was all right, but when we pressed the button we did not go to a floor.

The doors opened and all we could see was the works of the lift and darkness and red circles. I felt scared and everyone was silent. Then Mummy pressed the button again, but instead of moving, the lights went off. We were standing in darkness. There was a phone in the lift so Mum got the phone and called the people at the desk. They said, "We are coming, don't worry." So we waited for a while in silence.

When the door opened we had to jump onto a stool to get onto the floor. Now I never want to go in a lift again.

My Fear in Minorca

by
Rachael Monk

I'll never forget that day in Minorca when I was enjoying my holiday so much. When I woke up and yawned I did not know what I was in for.

"Mum," I asked. "Can we go and see a castle today?"

"OK," she said. "When we get downstairs, we'll ask the lady in the reception if she knows of anything."

The receptionist only had leaflets on one castle.

"Only one?" I asked.

"That's all I have," she said. "It's called Monte Torro."

My dad looked at the leaflet. "That looks nice," he said, and we got in the car.

Off we travelled and I read a book. About half an hour later I put down my book. We had come to a roundabout. There were two turn-offs, a long straight motorway and a crooked road with a steep hill at the end of it. I joked with my mum. "I'm glad we are not going THAT way!" I said, pointing at the crooked road. "But we are," said Mum.

I laughed, then I realised that my mum wasn't joking. We started to go along the crooked road. We got to the hill and started to drive up. I asked, "Why do they have a castle on a hill?"

55

Then I looked and, as we got higher, the road got narrower and the wall got lower. Suddenly the wall was gone! My dad froze, my mum screamed and I just wanted to be back on the ground. My dad said, "Shall we walk down or just turn around?" "Turn around," my mum and I replied.

If a car had come down the hill, it would have knocked us off the side, but I closed my eyes as tight as I could and crossed my fingers and toes. My mum said I could open my eyes and so I did. We were off the hill and on the way to a café. I could feel sweat oozing out of my body and I gave a sigh of relief that it was all over. When we got to the café I had a coke and my mum had a coffee. My dad also had a coffee and a big cigar.

But I must say, we never did get to the top of Monte Torro, and in a way I'm glad about it!

56

The Snow House

by

Curt Richardson

All I heard was banging. It was the kind of banging I always hear in the mornings. Doors opening and closing, cupboards slamming shut. I had a strange feeling about the day ahead – as my Mum and Dad had been arguing loudly the night before.

When I walked into the living room I noticed that some of my mum's ornaments were missing. I especially noticed my mum's snow dome had gone, the one I bought her from Birmingham with the little house and the snowman inside. I had always imagined living in the snow house. I never thought to ask where it was and I carried on into the kitchen.

My brother was dribbling so much Weetabix everywhere that the tray was like a Weetabix swamp. My mum was making her usual morning cup of tea. Everything seemed just as normal, but still I had a very strange feeling. I got dressed and walked over to my friend Mike's house. It was a windy day but the sun was shining. Half way to school we heard the bell ring. We ran as fast as we could with the wind blowing in our faces. Even though we ran we still arrived two minutes late. We weren't too worried about being late because our teacher, Mrs Gascoigne, was jolly and kind. I really liked that school and never once had a bad day. My friends were very special in and out of school.

Not saying good-bye was hard to cope with!

Anyway let's get back to the story. It was a normal Tuesday until half way through a video about Medusa. It's funny how I remember these things. The teacher called me over, a few of the children turned round to see what she wanted me for. I walked over to her and saw my mum. I felt confused, as it was only 2.15. Why was Mum picking me up at 2.15? Did I have an appointment with the doctor or dentist? All these questions were running through my mind, but my mum just looked blank – an expressionless face. Automatically I picked up my PE bag, coat and reading folder and headed towards the door, not daring to ask any questions. I headed off down the corridor and realised I would never see that school again, never say goodbye.

I walked to the end of the drive and saw two taxis. Why taxis? I noticed Jade first. She just sat there looking out of the window. Next to her sat my other sister, Jodie, and then there was little Charlie. My mum told me to go and sit in the first taxi so I did as she said, asking questions in my mind, not daring to ask for the truth. In the taxi I sat with my older sister.

I asked her where we were going and why? She just said Mum had asked her not to tell me. I was disappointed because she was keeping the truth from me, so I put my head in my hands and looked out of the window at the green fields and the old houses. It was a long journey for my first time in a taxi.

We turned a corner into a cul-de-sac and I saw a huge building with high green metal fences around it. It looked like a prison at first sight. We clambered out of the taxi and went through the huge gate. A small, chubby lady with curly, blonde hair came to welcome us. Doreen took us to a flat and told us there was food in the cupboard. She told us about activities we could do, and about the TV and video room.

The next two days were hard. I still didn't know where we were. On the third day my mum told me to sit down. She explained that she was having problems with my step-dad and we were at a refuge. A refuge was a place that you could go if your mum and dad were having a serious argument. It is a safe place where nobody can get in or out without having a special key. When she was telling me, I realised we were near a football stadium and I drifted off. Then suddenly it hit me, nothing was going to be the same again. Everything was changing.

The refuge was like living in an ordinary house, except it was smaller with more security and no outsiders were allowed in, not even friends. Staff were available twenty-four hours a day.

Next day Mum took me to see my new school. All I can remember is having to climb a long staircase to see the headteacher. As usual I just got on with it quietly, not asking too many questions. I sometimes felt how wonderful it would be to live in the little house in the snow dome, with a glass shell around, so nothing in your life could change.

We lived at the refuge for six months. I made some good friends at that school but never kept in touch with them. It was OK at the refuge, but I never talked to anybody about my problems. I think that is why I still get angry today. The refuge also went on trips to theme parks. These were happy times in a funny sort of way. After six months we had to move somewhere else and we ended up in another house. Moving areas again meant another new school. By now I had been to three different schools and moved twice in one year. The snow house with the shell around it seemed welcoming at this unstable time in my life.

We had a horrible time where we moved to, older children throwing stones, my little brother and sister were even bullied. I think this has added to why I am angry today. As you can guess we moved again, but I am a lot happier now and have started to talk about what happened on my journey. I still get angry sometimes but not as much as I used to. Things are going well at the moment, life is starting to feel safe again.

Just like the snow dome house.

The White Hart

by

Polly Noble

We were spending a camping holiday in Wales, at a sort of nature reserve. I was with my sister, Alice, and my mum.

The place was beautiful. Woodland and grassland, bracken in clumps, a tumbling stream, a huge lake, herds of deer and an old grey, gloomy castle. When we arrived I jumped for joy; it was almost too good to be true!

Every day we played and often I went to sketch the castle. Once, as I turned a corner, I saw a young doe from the deer herd, daintily nibbling a rose bush in the castle gardens. I was only a few feet away from it! I rushed back to tell Alice. Together, we crept back to the gardens, but the doe was nowhere in sight. So instead, we went to watch some Indian Runner ducks taking a bath in a large puddle, and we soon joined in!

Next morning it was hot and sunny. My sister and I went and splashed around in the crystal clear water of the stream. It started out with us dangling our legs from the log bridge, the spray from the waterfall soaking into our canvas shoes. Soon we were both sitting in the water, splashing each other! But we soon went into our tent and changed our clothes.

"Why don't you go to the park?" my mum asked. So we

started to walk down the track that led to the adventure playground. Trees made a bower of green above our heads, casting shadows on our path. We passed the far side of the shimmering lake and oh, how fresh and cool it looked! How I longed to plunge my feet into its silver depths! How I longed to splash my face with the shining water! But there was Alice to look after.

We walked a little further then . . . yes! We were at the adventure playground! Alice immediately ran over to the climbing frame and I went to have a go on the swings. I looked over to where the deer herd were grazing, around 500 yards away. The deer looked like blobs through the heat haze. There were lots of brownish blobs and . . . a white blob? It couldn't be! My imagination went wild. A dog? The herd would have scattered. A sheep? Not likely. A goat? Maybe. A girl was standing a small distance away from me. I walked over to her. "Excuse me, is that a goat?" I asked.

"Where?" she said.

"There. That white thing." I pointed to it.

"Wow!" exclaimed the girl. "You spotted the white hart."

"White hart?" I asked.

"It's an albino deer. People from all over the place come to see it, but they don't often see it because it hides. It's supposed to be a sign of good luck," she replied.

I looked over towards it. The sun shone on its gleaming white coat.

A sign of good luck.

Blackpool

by
Andrea Lancaster

As I awoke that Friday morning, I remembered it was the day I was going to Blackpool to dance with the Latin American team in a formation competition. I was going with my mam and younger brother Andrew for the weekend. We had already packed the night before, so when we got up we were almost ready to go.

When we got to the dance school we sat on the bus and waited for everyone to arrive. We set off early because it was a long journey and the band practice started at 10 o'clock. I sat there staring out of the window trying to hold in my excitement. At last, the bus started to move. Along the way, our mams started brushing up our hair really tightly into ponytails.

When we arrived in Blackpool we were a little early, so we had to queue up outside waiting for the Tower Ballroom to open. It was a really cold, miserable April day. Once inside we changed into our white T-shirts and blue skirts for the rehearsal. Before I knew it, I was standing on the floor, waiting for our music to play, poised ready to dance. I took a quick glance at Natasha and Emma who were holding our mascot – a little soft white bunny – by the ears. I thought this looked cruel, but I knew I must concentrate on what I was doing. Soon it came to the jive where I had to jump through my partner's legs on my heels. I had to do this with Ashleigh who was not much taller than me and I did not have much confidence in her. Luckily it went OK.

When we got off the floor we all gave each other a hug. When every team had danced, Dawn (our teacher) went to pick a piece of paper out of a hat to see in which order the teams would dance. When she returned and said we were team 'A' we were not very happy at having to be the first ones on the floor. We went to our hotel for lunch and when we had finished, we all put our make-up on and had our hair combed up into a bun which was excruciatingly painful! We set off for the Tower Ballroom.

Finally, the big moment arrived. For the second time we were walking down the steps to the huge dance floor and I had butterflies in my tummy. I saw the mams high up in the balcony, waving and then I decided I wanted to faint! I glanced at Natasha and Emma again and saw they were holding the bunny correctly which made me smile! We were a team of eight; four girls who danced as boys, wearing white shirts and black trousers, and four girls in beautiful pink dresses. We looked very smart indeed.

As the music began this time I felt more confident. We jived into the cha cha, melted into the rhumba, sprang into the samba and, finally, stamped into the impressive paso doble. With the girls stretched out on the floor and the boys standing behind us, we were ready to do the 'walk off'. After we had danced we hugged each other as we climbed back up the flights of stairs to the balcony where our mams were still cheering and clapping. My mam swept me off my feet with a big cuddle; she was so

pleased and proud of the way we had all danced. All we wanted to do then was go to Jungle Jim's play area, but we weren't allowed in case we got hurt and could not dance.

The most nerve-racking part of the event arrived as the announcement was made about which teams would dance in the final. The person reading out the team names said a letter . . .

but it was not letter A. My heart sank as I knew they were reading out the teams in alphabetical order and we had not gained a place in the final. I still hoped that they had missed us out and would say team A at the end, but no, they did not. We were all very disappointed because we felt we had danced well enough to be in the final. A few minutes later after we had changed into our ordinary clothes, we let our hair down as we clambered about in Jungle Jim's.

After a long time most of them made their way back to the hotel but my mam, brother and I and a few friends stayed to watch the older teams dance. When we eventually got back to the hotel, we got ready for bed and went back downstairs for a pyjama party with the grown-ups. We went to bed in the early hours of Saturday morning.

The weekend passed quickly and on the Saturday we went to The Sandcastle swimming pool which had four slides, a wave machine and a huge fountain. We had planned to spend the evening at the Pleasure Beach but unfortunately the police closed it as they were expecting football hooligan trouble. We returned to the hotel and we all played charades. All the children went to bed even later than the previous night – all in one room!

We finally got to the fairground on Sunday morning and for the first time went on a roller coaster, which I did not enjoy. My mam and Emma's mam went on the famous Pepsi Max roller coaster and they loved it. Mam wanted to go on again, and promised next time to keep her eyes open! We thoroughly enjoyed most of the different rides we tried. I would love to go back again.

I was so upset when I saw the bus arrive to take us home after our lunch. I did not want to go as I had had such a good time. It was the best weekend of my life!

The Unhappy Teddy Bear

by

Sophie Rayner

One hot day in Greece I was spying on a lizard on a rock when my mum called me in for a cold drink of lemonade. I was so hot that I wanted to go and sit in the shade outside. After a while I got bored so I went in and found my teddy bear. He was the first teddy bear that I had been given.

I got my bear, Fudge, when I was born. Fudge was the colour of sand from the beach and his eyes were light blue.

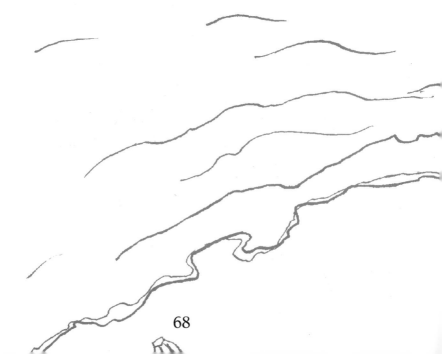

68

It was six o'clock on a dark Wednesday afternoon and I was running to the beach with my mum, dad and brothers. I laid Fudge on the soft sand.

The next day I was going home. I was so excited to be going back to my own bed the next sunny morning.

I stomped loudly in my villa room to check I had everything. I checked and checked. Suddenly I realised that I didn't have Fudge! My heart beat madly. I shouted for my mum.

"MUM, MUM, where's Fudge?"

I was running out of time. I chucked my bag down that was in the palm of my hand. Fudge was nowhere to be seen. I had to go back without him.

Slowly I calmed down. I felt lonely and empty inside without Fudge. On the plane I dreamed that Fudge was in my arms, but he wasn't.

When I got back home I decided that I should collect bears and so I did. I have millions of fluffy and china bears, but I still think about Fudge and I know he's in Greece, but where?

One day I will go to Greece and find him.

The Day I Wore High Heels

by

Anna Cartwright

I love dressing-up and pretending to be other people, sometimes a ruby-lipped pirate, sometimes a beautiful princess.

When I was three years old, my friend Georgia came round to my house to play with me and we both got dressed up in clothes from the dressing-up box. I chose a pair of my mother's high-heeled shoes to complete my high fashion outfit. I felt so very grown up as I walked around the upstairs bedrooms in one of my mother's dresses and a pair of my mother's shoes. I was so happy playing with my best friend that I completely forgot I wasn't wearing my normal trainers.

I took a step onto the stairs when BANG! I tripped and BUMP! BUMP! BUMP! I went all the way down to the bottom! OUCH! I was really scared and my arm HURT and hung down in a funny way. I did not know it then but I had broken my arm. I sat at the bottom of the stairs and I cried. My friend came running down the stairs and she kept asking me if I was all right. My mother, hearing the noise, came and gave me a cuddle. She wrapped me in her red shawl with flowers on it and put me in the car.

Dad drove me to hospital.

When I got to the hospital a nurse looked at my arm and took me to have some X-ray pictures. The doctor told me I had broken it badly and I had to stay in hospital for thirteen days. My arm was in a big plaster and I had to have it in traction while it mended.

In the children's ward I met a very nice lady who came to paint my face lots of times. My favourite face painting session was when she painted it blue, with red lips and with little flowers all round my face. Mummy came to visit me every day and brought me lots and lots of sweets.

The Day I Stopped Roller-Blading

by
Jack Swain

Roller-blades. They were my main thought. A flashy new pair of roller-blades. I had purchased them from a shop the day before. They were dark blue with yellow buckles and black wheels. They had the words BRAVOBLADE in silver, italic writing on the back, and the best thing was – we were going to Hyde Park to try them out.

But I couldn't wait that long. I crept cautiously and silently, in fear of being caught by my parents at six in the morning, to a cupboard in their room. I took out a box and opened it. Inside, were my roller-blades. Excitedly, I put them on and started roller-blading across the room.

Suddenly, I tripped. My body was thrown across the room and I hit my chin sharply on a chair leg. Blood oozed out of my chin onto my clothes and, eventually, onto the floor.

My dad ran over and peered at my gaping chin. He muttered sleepily, "I think he needs stitches." Mum, who can't stand to look at blood or anything gruesome, pulled the duvet over her head and hid.

I cried all the way to the hospital with painful sobs, clasping a tissue to my chin. My chin had a huge dent in it, and was continually bleeding. We entered the Minor Injuries Unit of St

Charles' Hospital and sat down. Dad went to find a nurse, while my sister feebly tried to dab at my wound. She wasn't much use, though, as she refused to look at it and kept saying she was going to faint.

Dad soon came back with a small, rather grim looking nurse, who I took an instant dislike to. She told me to lift my chin up, so I did. To my surprise, she squeezed it. I let out an agonised yell.

Then my dad and the 'torturer' nurse held a whispered conversation on the other side of the room. I caught only one word, a word that seemed to freeze my entire body and go up my spine like a thunderbolt. The word was STITCHES!

"No," I screamed. "Can't I just have a plaster or something? I don't want any stupid stitches!"

Dad smiled a bit and bent down to talk to me. "If you had a plaster, it wouldn't heal properly. With stitches in, your chin will mend quickly and well."

"Will it hurt?" I asked, hopefully.

"No," he said. Later, I realised that whatever I had asked him he would have said, "No," or whatever answer would reassure me that I'd be all right.

I was led to a room, like a lamb to a sacrificial altar. It had a table, a bed and a lot of odd looking instruments lying around. The little, grim nurse left the room. Another chubby, happier nurse with springy, frizzy, orange hair came in pushing a trolley on which was a needle, some special sort of thread and tissues.

"Hello, I'm Jenny. What did you do to yourself?"

"He was roller-blading inside the house," sneered my know-it-all sister.

"As one does," added Dad, rather pleased with his joke. So much for family support.

"Well, what a coincidence," said the springy-haired Jenny.

"Only two weeks ago, my boy was roller-skating in the house and he fell down the stairs. He was screaming and hollering the place down. I'm sorry, but the gash in your chin is too deep to put a bandage on, so I'm going to have to give you . . ."

She paused and inspected my chin gently, ". . . six stitches. Now, if I ask you whether it hurts or not during the surgery, wink with your left eye if it hurts, and with your right, if it doesn't."

The nurse gave me this information with a jolly tone in her voice, but it didn't make me feel any better. Dad whispered in my ear, "If you stay still and don't move, I'll buy you twenty packs of football stickers."

This was an offer too good to refuse. I sat rigid in the chair with my chin proudly pointing upwards, so the jolly nurse could stitch it up. She put the stitches in quickly and efficiently, and all I felt was a small stinging sensation.

After about a minute of stitching, the nurse backed away and stared at her work on my chin. "There, all done," she said. "You can go home now."

I was astonished. It was all over so soon. A bit embarrassed, I regretted all the fuss I'd made. If I had known it would have been as painless and brief as this I would have walked into the room and got it over with. Just like that. No bribing was needed, really. Still, it was worth it, just to get twenty packs of football stickers.

Of course, there were bad things about stitches and quite a few restrictions. For instance, I was not allowed to wash my face, or if I did, I had to make sure I didn't get my chin wet. Also, I couldn't play any sports at school, as something, or someone, might come into contact with my chin.

It was ten days before I had my stitches taken out, and when the time finally came, I was glad. I was getting a bit fed up with not being able to do anything.

When I went back to the hospital, with my mum this time, I was perfectly happy, mainly because I was missing some school. Besides, I knew it wouldn't be that bad really.

Unfortunately, I found out that the small, grim nurse was going to remove my stitches. Now my high spirits dropped. I was taken into the room, just like before, but this time the 'torturer' nurse wasn't putting stitches in, but taking them out with a rather large pair of tweezers.

She roughly hooked one of the stitches with the cold, metal tweezers and yanked abruptly, so the stitch was jerked out. Horribly, she did this with all six, until finally, they were all ripped out. Those two minutes were a living hell. But at least it was over. That was the main thing.

After that nasty experience, I took a vow never, ever to roller-blade again.

Well, inside the house, anyway!

Authors and their schools

Rachael Monk 55
Thorpedene GM Junior School, Shoeburyness

Polly Noble 61
Farmborough VC Primary School, Bath

Shankara Oakes 54
Town Close House Pre-Prep School, Norwich

Craig Parry 29
Cwmdu C in W School, Crickhowell

Scott Phillips 43
Greenleas Lower School, Linslade, Leighton Buzzard

Ellie Ragdale 32
De Vere County Primary School, Castle Hedingham

Sophie Rayner – *winner year 4* 68
De Vere County Primary School, Castle Hedingham

Curt Richardson – *winner year 6* 57
Sunnyside Primary School, Chilwell Beeston, Nottingham

James Richardson 20
Greenleas Lower School, Linslade, Leighton Buzzard

Tom Risdon 38
Colet Court, Barnes, London

Huw Silk 36
Cwmdu C in W School, Crickhowell

Sarah Smith 16
Linslade Middle School, Leighton Buzzard

Jack Swain 72
Colet Court, Barnes, London

CAMBRIDGE
Young
Writers
award

The Competition

The Cambridge Young Writers Award was launched in January 1999 in the National Year of Reading, as a joint initiative by Cambridge University and Cambridge University Press. It was open to all UK children from Year 2 to Year 6, who were asked to write about a significant event in their own lives and to produce a well-crafted, believable story which moved the reader. The response was terrific and *I'm Telling You!* is the result: the judges' selection of 25 excellent and contrasting stories.

The Judges

The judging panel was chaired by Professor Dame Gillian Beer, former Chair of The Booker Prize judges; the other judges were Michael Rosen, well-known broadcaster and children's author, Julia Eccleshare, Children's Books Editor of the *Guardian*, Jackie Kay, prize-winning children's poet and Richard Brown, children's author.

Interest at the Highest Level

The CYWA prizes were presented by David Blunkett, MP. At the award ceremony, Mr Blunkett announced his support for the competition and his strong personal commitment to fostering creative writing among children.

Royalties to Charity

All royalties from the sale of *I'm Telling You!*
will be donated to the
Leukaemia Research Fund,
43 Great Ormond St,
London WC1N 3JJ.

To find out how to enter the Cambridge Young Writers Award contact the Project Manager,
Rosemary Hayes
Durhams Farmhouse, Butcher's Hill,
Ickleton, Saffron Walden,
Essex CB10 1SR.
Phone and fax: 01799 531192
e-mail: r.hayes@btinternet.com